Piglets

Alex Kuskowski

A Division of ABDO

ABDO
Publishing Company

Consulting Editor, Diane Craig, M.A./Reading Specialist

visit us at www.abdopublishing.com

Published by ABDO Publishing Company, a division of ABDO, P.O. Box 398166, Minneapolis, Minnesota 55439. Copyright © 2014 by Abdo Consulting Group, Inc. International copyrights reserved in all countries. No part of this book may be reproduced in any form without written permission from the publisher. SandCastle™ is a trademark and logo of ABDO Publishing Company.

Printed in the United States of America, North Mankato, Minnesota
062013
012014

 PRINTED ON RECYCLED PAPER

Editor: Liz Salzmann
Content Developer: Alex Kuskowski
Cover and Interior Design and Production: Mighty Media, Inc.
Photo Credits: Shutterstock, Thinkstock

Library of Congress Cataloging-in-Publication Data
Kuskowski, Alex.
 Piglets / by Alex Kuskowski.
    pages cm. -- (Baby animals)
 ISBN 978-1-61783-839-2
1. Piglets--Juvenile literature. I. Title.
 SF395.5.K87 2013
 636.4'07--dc23
                        2012049956

SandCastle™ Level: Beginning

SandCastle™ books are created by a team of professional educators, reading specialists, and content developers around five essential components—phonemic awareness, phonics, vocabulary, text comprehension, and fluency—to assist young readers as they develop reading skills and strategies and increase their general knowledge. All books are written, reviewed, and leveled for guided reading, early reading intervention, and Accelerated Reader® programs for use in shared, guided, and independent reading and writing activities to support a balanced approach to literacy instruction. The SandCastle™ series has four levels that correspond to early literacy development. The levels are provided to help teachers and parents select appropriate books for young readers.

| Emerging Readers (no flags) | Beginning Readers (1 flag) | Transitional Readers (2 flags) | Fluent Readers (3 flags) |

Contents

Piglets

A baby pig is a piglet.
Piglets live on farms.
Some people have
piglets as pets.

Piglets are born in a **litter**. They have many brothers and sisters.

Jack feeds his piglet. Newborn piglets drink milk. Older piglets eat grass, roots, and fruit.

Emma's piglet is two months old. In four more months the piglet will be fully grown.

Lauren's piglet **snuggles** in the hay. Hay keeps piglets warm.

Max the piglet rolls in the mud. Mud helps piglets stay cool on hot days.

Piglets love to play together. The piglets play on a farm.

Ellie pets Polly. Polly's coat has **bristles** that feel **rough**.

Piglets are smart. Colin teaches his piglets how to race.

Did You Know?

▶ Piglets have a great sense of smell. Some people train them to find **truffles**.

▶ Piglets cannot see very well.

▶ Piglets do not sweat.

▶ Piglets can get sunburned.

Piglet Quiz

Read each sentence below. Then decide whether it is true or false.

1. Piglets are born in a **litter**.

2. Newborn piglets eat grass, roots, and fruit.

3. Mud helps piglets stay cool.

4. Piglets have **bristles**.

5. Piglets are not smart animals.

Glossary

bristle – a short, stiff hair or something similar to a hair.

litter – a group of baby animals, such as piglets, born at the same time.

rough – not smooth or soft.

snuggle – to curl up in a comfortable or cozy place.

truffle – a mushroom that grows in the ground near trees and is used in cooking.